Learning to Write
Adverbs

WEIGL PUBLISHERS INC.

Published by Weigl Publishers Inc.
350 5th Avenue, Suite 3304, PMB 6G
New York, NY 10118-0069

Website: www.weigl.com
Copyright ©2010 WEIGL PUBLISHERS INC.

All of the Internet URLs given in the book were valid at the time of publication. However, due to the dynamic nature of the Internet, some addresses may have changed, or sites may have ceased to exist since publication. While the author and publisher regret any inconvenience this may cause readers, no responsibility for any such changes can be accepted by either the author or the publisher.

Library of Congress Cataloging-in-Publication Data

Lambert, Deborah.
  Adverbs / Deborah Lambert.
      p. cm. -- (Learning to write)
  Includes webliography and index.
  ISBN 978-1-60596-050-0 (hard cover : alk. paper) -- ISBN 978-1-60596-051-7 (soft cover : alk. paper)
  1. English language--Adverb--Juvenile literature. I. Title.
  PE1325.L36 2010
  428.2--dc22
                                     2009001957

Printed in China
1 2 3 4 5 6 7 8 9 0 13 12 11 10 09

Editor: Deborah G. Lambert
Design: Terry Paulhus

Photograph Credits

Weigl acknowledges Getty images as its image supplier for this title.

Other photograph credits include: Alamy: page 14; Janet Feathers: page 15.

All of the internet URLs given in the book were valid at the time of publication. However, due to the dynamic nature of the internet, some addresses may have changed, or sites may have ceased to exist since publication. While the author and publisher regret any inconvenience this may cause readers, no responsibility for any such changes can be accepted by either the author or the publisher.

Every reasonable effort has been made to trace ownership and to obtain permission to reprint copyright material. The publishers would be pleased to have any errors or omissions brought to their attention so that they may be corrected in subsequent printings.

Table of Contents

What is an Adverb?

An adverb is a describing word. It is a part of speech that describes a **verb**. It can also describe an **adjective** or another adverb.

An adverb can be placed anywhere in a sentence. It can start or end a sentence. The adverb can be placed between the **noun** or **pronoun** and the verb. The easiest adverbs to identify are those that end in *ly*.

In the following paragraph about Navajo homes, the adverbs are shaded red. The Navajo belong to one of the largest American Indian tribes in the United States.

*The Navajo built homes called **hogans**. They thought carefully about where to build each hogan. They would not build on gravesites, old battlegrounds, or areas where trees had been struck by lightning. Usually, the Navajo made their hogans with stone and hardened clay brick. Today, some Navajo still live in these hogans.*

In this paragraph, the adverb "carefully" describes the verb *thought*, and the adverb "usually" describes the verb *made*. These adverbs end with *ly*. The adverb "still" is an adverb that does not end in *ly*. Which verb does it describe?

Finding Adverbs

Some adverbs have been used in this paragraph about the foods that the Navajo eat. Find these adverbs, and make a list of them in your notebook.

*For the Navajo, food certainly had a special meaning. It was always used to welcome guests. This was how they joyfully gave thanks for their belongings. The Navajo mainly cooked from memory. They mostly used their fingers and hands to measure the **ingredients** they needed to cook their foods. The Navajo did not have ovens. They easily prepared their meals over an open fire.*

To learn more about the Navajo, go to **http://inkido.indiana.edu/w310work/ romac/navajo.htm**. As you read about the Navajo, find other examples of adverbs used to describe how they live.

Identifying Types of Adverbs

There are many types of adverbs. Some describe the manner, place, or time of an action. This means they tell *how, where,* and *when* something happens.

Adverbs that tell *how* something happens can include words such as *carefully, quickly, quietly, easily, badly, simply, fast,* and *well.*

Adverbs that tell *where* something happens can include words such as *there, here, anywhere, everywhere, nowhere, around, away, inside, outside, toward, on, up, over, down, along, across, behind,* and *nearby.*

Those that tell *when* something happens can include words such as *yesterday, today, soon, after, now, while, next, since, later, last, every, usually, sometimes, never, often, until, always, still, just, during, rarely, finally, then,* and *throughout.*

In these three sentences about the Pueblo, each type of adverb is shaded red. Using the examples of adverbs on this page to help you, name the types of adverbs used in the sentences.

The Pueblo treated strangers well and tried to speak nicely to each other.

Today, most Pueblo live in cities.

When the ladders were brought inside, the pueblo village was protected from intruders.

To learn more about the Pueblo, go to **www.bigorrin.org/pueblo_kids.htm**. Look for the adverbs used on this site. How many types did you find?

Selecting Types of Adverbs

These paragraphs describe the dances of the Sioux. Find the adverbs in the sentences, and list them in your notebook.

In 1889, an Indian named Wovoka found a new religion called the Ghost Dance. This religion quickly spread to the Sioux. Elaborate dances and special songs are certainly important parts of the Ghost Dance.

*Dance festivals called **wacipi** began in the 1930s. Today, wacipi is a celebration of people coming together for dancing, music, crafts, food, and fun. Dancers gracefully move to the drumbeat. They compete for prizes while dancing to the drums.*

How many adverbs did you find? To learn more about Sioux culture, go to **www.nativeamericans.com/Sioux.htm**. Look for more adverbs in these descriptions, and add them to your list.

Learning about Adverbs of Manner

An adverb of manner tells *how* something happens. In a sentence, it can be placed right before or after the action verb. Some adverbs of manner can also be placed at the end of sentences. To make sure that the adverb in a sentence is an adverb of manner, you must always ask a question about the action, starting with *how*.

In these sentences about the Ojibwa, adverbs of manner are used.

When performing the Grass Dance, the Ojibwa men gracefully swayed their bodies.

Usually, Ojibwa men and women perform traditional dances separately.

After the Ojibwa harvested wild rice, it was well dried, then boiled, and served with meat or fowl.

In the first sentence, if we ask how the Ojibwa men sway their bodies, we will get the answer "gracefully." The word "gracefully" is the adverb of manner in the first sentence. Next, ask how Ojibwa men and women perform traditional dances. The adverb of manner is "separately."

Try asking *how* the wild rice was dried in the last sentence. What is the adverb of manner?

Identifying Adverbs of Manner

The wigwam is the name given to the type of house in which the Ojibwa lived. A wigwam is shaped like a **dome**. It is usually covered with **rush mats** and birch bark.

The following paragraph describes how the Ojibwa built wigwams. Adverbs of manner have been used to tell how the actions in the sentences are happening. For example, if we ask how wigwams were built, we learn that the adverb of manner is "easily." Find the other adverbs of manner in this paragraph, and make a list of them in your notebook.

Wigwams were built easily. They were well suited to groups like the Ojibwa. To begin building the wigwams, the men set poles solidly in the ground. Then, they bent the poles and quickly tied them to make a dome-shaped frame. Next, the women neatly covered the frame with rush mats. They then lay birch-bark sheets over the mats carefully. The birch-bark sheets overlap like shingles on a roof. This successfully prevents rain and wind from entering the wigwam. Wigwams keep the Ojibwa warm and dry.

To read more about the Ojibwa, go to **www.bigorrin.org/chippewa_kids.htm**. Look for more adverbs that tell how the actions in the sentences are happening. Add them to your list.

Learning about Adverbs of Place

An adverb of place tells *where* something happens. It is most often placed after the action verb in a sentence. Some adverbs of place can also be placed at the end of sentences.

To make sure that the adverb in a sentence is an adverb of place, you must always ask a question about the action, starting with *where*.

In these sentences about the Cherokee, adverbs of place are used. In the second sentence, if you ask "where the Cherokee spent most of their summer," you will get the answer "outside." The word "outside" is the adverb of place of the second sentence.

Try asking questions starting with *where* for the actions in the other sentences about the Cherokee. What are the adverbs of place in these sentences?

The Cherokee stayed there for many generations.

Many Cherokee spent most of the summer outside, so they did not need complex homes.

In Cherokee society, when two people got married, they lived near the wife's family.

To learn more about the Cherokee, go to **www.bigorrin.org/ cherokee_kids.htm**. Using questions starting with *where*, find more adverbs of place on this site.

Identifying Adverbs of Place

Read these paragraphs about the houses built by the Pueblo. Adverbs of place have been used to tell where the actions in the sentences are happening. Find these adverbs, and make a list of them in your notebook.

*Pueblo houses look like apartments. They have **hinged** doors and glass windows, which face toward a central **plaza**. The solid mud walls and roofs of Pueblo houses are thick. This keeps the houses cool inside, even when it is hot outside.*

The Pueblo placed large logs called vigas *across the top of their houses to support the flat roofs. They took vigas from the mountain forests nearby.*

To read more on Pueblo houses, go to **www.mce.k12tn.net/indians/ reports2/pueblo.htm**. On this website, look for more adverbs that tell where actions are happening in the sentences. Add them to your list.

Learning about Adverbs of Time

An adverb of time tells when something happens. It can also tell for how long or how often something happens. An adverb of time is most often placed after the action verb in a sentence. Some adverbs of time can also begin or end sentences.

To make sure that the adverb in a sentence is an adverb of time, you must always ask a question about the action, starting with *when*.

In these paragraphs about the foods that the Cherokee ate, some adverbs of time are used. Try asking questions starting with *when* for the action in each sentence about the Cherokee. What are the adverbs of time in this paragraph?

Corn was a very important part of the Cherokee diet. They used corn to create many different foods. Sometimes, they ate fresh corn. They also added fruits to their diet. The women often dried the fruits before serving them to their families.

Kanuchi *was a* **delicacy** *among the Cherokee. Kanuchi was prepared by pounding hickory nuts into a paste. After this paste was rolled into balls, it was boiled in water. It was then dissolved into a liquid as thick as cream. Kanuchi is still prepared today.*

Identifying Adverbs of Time

These paragraphs are about the tools used by the Navajo. Read these paragraphs carefully. Then, make a list of all the adverbs of time you can find.

Many tools, such as **ladles**, spoons, and dishes were used everyday by the Navajo. These tools were often made from dried **gourds** or carved from wood.

The Navajo also used tools to harvest and prepare corn. They dried the corn to preserve it for use throughout the year. The corn was placed in a pot of water over hot coals overnight. Then, the corn kernels were scraped from the cob and placed in the Sun to dry the next morning. Finally, the Navajo used two pieces of stone to grind the dried kernels into cornmeal.

The Navajo used tools to make silver jewelry. They carved designs into a soft rock. Then, they used the carved rock as mold to **cast** silver. Navajo always used **awls** to punch designs into the silver pieces. Later, they used fine files and other tools to make more markings and smaller pieces of metal.

Where Do They Belong?

In learning to use adverbs, you should be able to identify each type. In this paragraph about the type of homes built by the Iroquois, the adverbs have been shaded red.

*The type of houses built by the Iroquois were called **longhouses**. To build a longhouse, the Iroquois men skillfully tied long wooden poles to form arches. Then, they placed the poles lengthwise to connect and support the arches. Longhouses were usually between 60 and 220 feet (18 and 67 meters) long.*

Inside, the longhouse was divided into apartments. The Iroquois built platforms along the interior walls of the longhouse. As longhouse dwellers, the Iroquois used their space well. They neatly hung items, such as snowshoes, on walls.

Each of the adverbs shown belongs to one of the types you learned in this book. This chart shows where some of them belong.

ADVERBS		
Manner	**Place**	**Time**
skillfully	inside, along	Then

On a sheet of paper, complete the chart by placing the other adverbs in the paragraph in their correct columns. Remember to use questions starting with *how*, *where*, and *when* to help you identify the type of adverb.

Grouping Adverbs

In these paragraphs about the clothing worn by the Cherokee, some adverbs have been used. In your notebook, draw a table like the one on this page. Then, place each adverb from these paragraphs in its proper column. Three examples are done for you.

European settlers brought many types of clothing to the Cherokee. After the Cherokee were removed from their land, they chose one unique style of clothing.

When they were forced to leave their homes, Cherokee families had to move away without their belongings and clothing. As a result, the women did not have scissors to use for sewing. Instead, pieces of material were carefully torn from fabric and creatively sewn into dresses. These were called tear dresses. These dresses were made so they would not get in the way while the women worked around the house or in the fields. The tear dresses are still worn today.

ADVERBS		
Manner	**Place**	**Time**
carefully	away	After

Using Adverbs to Create Sentences

Adverbs give more information about how, where, and when something happens. They make sentences more interesting. You can use adverbs to create your own sentences about things that are happening around you.

Start by making a list of the adverbs from the following paragraph describing how the Pueblo make their pottery. The adverbs are shaded red. This paragraph tells how the Pueblo make pottery.

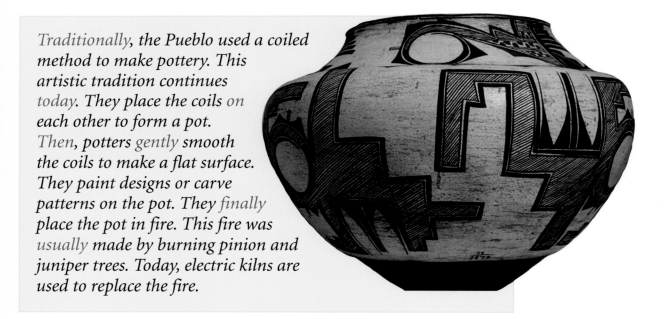

Traditionally, the Pueblo used a coiled method to make pottery. This artistic tradition continues today. They place the coils on each other to form a pot. Then, potters gently smooth the coils to make a flat surface. They paint designs or carve patterns on the pot. They finally place the pot in fire. This fire was usually made by burning pinion and juniper trees. Today, electric kilns are used to replace the fire.

Now, write four sentences describing how the Pueblo make pottery. Use the adverbs on the list you made. One has been done for you. The adverb is shaded red.

Today, the Pueblo are using a coiled method to make pottery.

Creating Your Own Sentences Using Adverbs

No adverbs have been used in these sentences about the Iroquois. Rewrite the sentences, and include the most suitable adverbs to describe the action verbs. You can use the lists on page 6 to help you.

The medicine wheel was used in celebrations.

Medicine and religion were tied in the Iroquois culture.

The Iroquois ate one meal a day.

The Iroquois diet consisted of corn, beans, and squash.

Iroquois women wore cloth dresses, which were decorated with porcupine quills or beads.

The women wore leggings underneath a dress or skirt.

Use the Internet, or visit the library to find more information about the Iroquois. Then, in your notebook, write five of your own sentences describing their way of life. Use the types of adverbs explained in this book in your sentences.

Tools for Learning about Adverbs

What did you learn? Look at the topics in the "Skills" column. Compare them to the page number in the "Page" column. Review the content you learned about adverbs by reading the "Content" column below.

SKILLS	CONTENT	PAGE
Defining an adverb	Navajo homes, Navajo foods	4–5
Identifying types of adverbs	Pueblo, Sioux dances	6–7
Learning about adverbs of manner	Ojibwa, Ojibwa homes	8–9
Learning about adverbs of place	Cherokee, Pueblo homes	10–11
Learning about adverbs of time	Cherokee foods, Navajo tools	12–13
Grouping adverbs according to type	Iroquois homes, Cherokee clothing	14–15
Using adverbs	Pueblo pottery, Iroquois	16–17

LEARNING TO WRITE

Practice Writing Your Own Paragraphs Using Adverbs

Many legends have been written about American Indians. The Hopi tells one of these legends about how the great chiefs made the Moon and the Sun. To read this legend, go to **www.indigenouspeople.net/howthegr.htm**.

1.   Read this legend carefully. Then, make a list of all the adverbs used.

2.   Use the adverbs from your list to write two paragraphs about how you think the great chiefs made the Moon or the Sun.

The following are pictures of the Hopi. The Hopi are the Indians of Northeastern Arizona. They and their ancestors have lived there for thousands of years.

Put Your Knowledge to Use

Many stories have been told about the chiefs of American Indian groups. Two of these stories are about Crazy Horse and American Horse of the Sioux.

For the story about Crazy Horse, go to **www.indigenouspeople.net/ crazyhor.htm**. The story about American Horse can be found at **www. snowwowl.com/nativeleaders/americanhorse.html**.

Read these stories. Then, in your own own words, write a story about how one of these chiefs helped others to survive. Use the types of adverbs that you have learned in this book to write your story.

Crazy Horse was a Sioux Chief of the Oglala. He was a warrior who resisted the invasion of the Great Plains.

American Horse (right) was also a Sioux Chief of the Oglala. He was one of the earliest supporters of education for American Indians.

Use the Internet, or visit the library to find more information about American Indian groups in the United States, not discussed in this book. In your notebook, try writing a story about one of the American Indian groups you chose. Use the types of adverbs that you learned in this book in your story.

You can start with some information about the Apache at **www.bigorrin.org/ apache_kids.htm**.

EXPANDED CHECKLIST

Reread your sentences, paragraphs, or stories to make sure that you have all of the following.

- ☑ Adverbs that tell *how* things happened or are happening

- ☑ Adverbs that tell *where* things happened or are happening

- ☑ Adverbs that tell *when* things happened or are happening

Other Parts of Speech

You have now learned the tools for using adverbs. You can use your knowledge of adverbs to write clear and interesting sentences, paragraphs, or stories. There are four other parts of speech. You can use some of the same tools you learned in this book to use these other parts of speech. The chart below shows the other parts of speech and their key features.

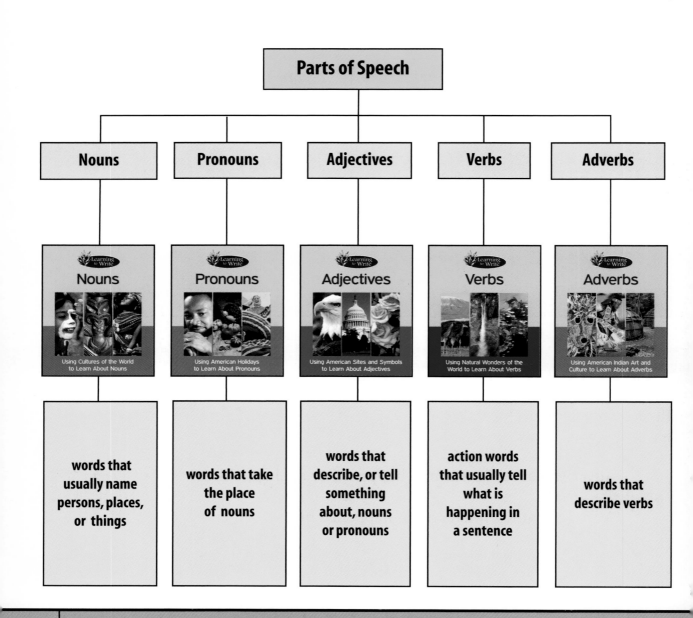

Parts of Speech				
Nouns	**Pronouns**	**Adjectives**	**Verbs**	**Adverbs**
words that usually name persons, places, or things	words that take the place of nouns	words that describe, or tell something about, nouns or pronouns	action words that usually tell what is happening in a sentence	words that describe verbs

Further Research

Books

Many books provide information on adverbs. To learn more about how to use different types of adverbs, you can borrow books from the library. To learn more about American Indian art and culture, try reading these books.

Lomberg, Michelle. *The Iroquois*. New York, NY: Weigl Publishers Inc., 2004.

Lomberg, Michelle. *The Ojibwa*. New York, NY: Weigl Publishers Inc., 2004.

Craats, Rennay. *The Navajo*. New York, NY: Weigl Publishers Inc., 2004.

Websites

On the Internet, you can type terms, such as "adverbs" or "types of adverbs," into the search bar of your Web browser, and click the search button. It will take you to a number of sites with this information.

Read more about American Indian art and culture at **www.native-languages.org/kids.htm** and **www.americanindians.com**.

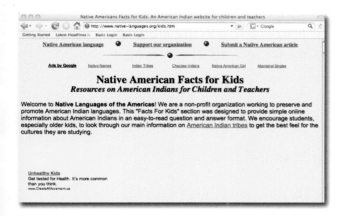

Glossary

adjective: a part of speech that describes, or tells something about, a noun or pronoun

awls: sharp, pointed tools used for piercing holes in soft materials

cast: to pour hot metal into a mold and allow it to cool and harden

delicacy: a special food

dome: a rounded vault forming the roof of a building or structure, usually with a circular base

gourds: fleshy, large fruit with a hard skin

hinged: movable joint on which a door swings as it opens and closes

hogans: pyramid-shaped homes with five to eight sides

ingredients: foods or substances mixed together to make a particular dish

ladles: large, long-handled spoons with a cup-shaped bowl used for serving soup, stew, or sauce

longhouses: long, narrow houses made of wood and bark

noun: the part of speech that is usually used to name a person, place, or thing

plaza: a central area in a village, which is used for gathering, working, and playing

pronoun: the part of speech that is used instead of a noun

rush mats: mats made from branches of bull rush plants

verb: the part of speech that describes what a noun or pronoun is doing in a sentence

wacipi: American Indian dance festivals involving singing, dancing, and drumming

Index